Oracle Asset (Functional) Practice Questions for Interviews and Certification Examination (Release 11i and 12)

ERP Gold

Printed in the United States of America

First Printing: October 2010

ISBN - 1456311581

Oracle Asset (Functional) Practice Questions for Interviews and Certification Examination

(Release 11i and 12)

Question 1 of 150

You are implementing Oracle Asset for your client, and they want to separately track and manage detachable Asset components, while still automatically grouping them to their parent Asset, how do you approach this?

A. Oracle can track and manage detachable Asset components but cannot automatically group them to their parent Asset.
B. By specifying a rule in the Asset Categories window by which Oracle Assets defaults the life for a sub component Asset based on the category and the parent Asset life.
C. This is a gap that Oracle Asset cannot address.
D. Oracles automatically tracks and manage detachable Asset components once the track as subcomponent button is checked in the view subcomponent window.

Question 2 of 150

Which of the following allows you to control access to Oracle Assets through responsibilities that you create and assign to users of the system?

A. Security group
B. Security profile
C. Profile Option

D. System Control

Question 3 of 150

Revalue Assets to adjust the value of your
capitalized Assets in a highly inflationary
economy. You can revalue all the following except?

A. All categories in a book.
B. All Assets in a category
C. Imported Assets
D. Individual Assets

Question 4 of 150

The Mass Revaluation process uses price indexes to
revalue Assets.

A. True
B. False

Question 5 of 150

To use the Physical Inventory feature, you must
first take physical inventory of your Assets and the
following information about your Assets is

required except?

A. The location
B. The number of units
C. A unique identifier, which can be either the Asset number, tag number, or serial number.
D. Asset category

Question 6 of 150

Oracle Assets sends journal entries directly to the following tables except?

A. GL_JE_LINES
B. GL_JE_COLUMN
C. GL_JE_BATCHES
D. GL_JE_HEADERS

Question 7 of 150

Which queue will the Mass Additions Post program select as mass additions lines to be processed?

A. Cost Adjustment
B. Control
C. Merged
D. On Hold

Which of the following statements is not true about a CIP Asset cost?

A. Oracle Assets automatically updates the cost to the sum of the invoice line costs after you add invoice lines to a CIP Asset using the Mass Additions process.

B. Oracle Assets defaults a cost of zero for construction-in-process (CIP) Assets and you can change it later.

C. You can also change the cost of a CIP Asset manually by entering non-invoiced items or transferring invoice lines between Assets in the Source Lines window.

D. All the above.

Question 9 of 150

_____ is used to determine whether Assets should be depreciated, the type of depreciation method to use and Asset life term?

A. Depreciation bonus
B. Depreciation method
C. Depreciation rules
D. Depreciation calendar.

Question 10 of 150

Oracle Assets uses the Major Category segment for capital budgeting?

A. False
B. True

Question 11 of 150

Oracle Assets automatically perform the same transaction on a sub component Asset when you perform it on the parent Asset.

A. False
B. True

Question 12 of 150

If the FA: Use Workflow Account Generation profile option is set to No, which of the following must be set up?

A. Prorate and Retirement Conventions
B. Sub-ledger Accounting
C. Asset Category
D. Account generator

Which of the following is not true?

A. Changing the location or employee information, however, has no financial impact because Oracle Assets uses them solely for property tax and responsibility reporting.
B. Changing the expense account has a financial impact, since Oracle Assets creates journal entries for depreciation expense to the general ledger using the account.
C. You can transfer an Asset between employees, expense accounts, and locations.
D. You can transfer an Asset between employees, projects, and locations.

Which of the following statements is not true?

A. You cannot run depreciation projections for several books if all books have the same Account flex-field structure.
B. You need only one copy of Oracle Assets to implement multiple ledgers.
C. If you want to transfer Assets that are in different corporate depreciation books, you must retire the Asset from one depreciation book and add it to the other.
D. You can use Oracle Assets with multiple

ledgers, within a single Oracle Asset.

Question 15 of 150

Which of the following is not a depreciation method in Oracle Assets?

A. Life-based
B. Fixed rate
C. Price-based rate
D. Units of production

Question 16 of 150

Which of the following is a required segment in the Location Key Flex-field?

A. Minor
B. State
C. Major
D. None of the above

Question 17 of 150

Which depreciation method depreciates an Asset based on quantity of that Asset used during the accounting period?

A. Units of production
B. Work in production
C. Work in process
D. Units in process

Question 18 of 150

Flat-rate depreciation methods determine the depreciation rate using fixed rates, including all the following except?

A. Adjusting rate
B. Bonus rate
C. Year of life
D. Basic rate

Question 19 of 150

Which function can be performed in Mass Additions window?

A. Add to Assets
B. Merge
C. Split
D. All the above

Which of the following is not true about Oracle Asset?

A. You can update the revaluation reserve after the period you added the Asset.
B. If you try to revalue the Asset cost above the ceiling, Oracle Assets uses the revaluation
C. You cannot claim an Investment Tax Credit on an Asset unless it is using a life-based depreciation method.
D. Net Book Value = Current Cost - Total Reserve (Accumulated Depreciation + Bonus Reserve)

Question 21 of 150

You load your physical inventory data into Oracle Assets using all the following methods except?

A. Physical Inventory Entries window
B. Use the Mass Addition interface import program
C. Use the Record Physical Inventory process in the Applications Desktop Integrator (ADI).
D. Use SQL*Loader to import physical inventory data from a non-Oracle file system.

Question 22 of 150

Which of the following depreciation book must be defined before you can perform mass depreciation adjustments?

A. Budget book
B. Tax book
C. Corporate book
D. None of the above

Question 23 of 150

If you are using Multiple Reporting Currencies (MRC), you can only run the Calculate
Gains and Losses and depreciation programs using which of the following responsibilities?

A. MRC primary responsibility
B. General Ledger super-User responsibility
C. Fixed Asset responsibility
D. All the above

Question 24 of 150

Which of the following is true about oracle Asset close process?

A. You can reopen closed Oracle Asset period

provided that the General Ledger period is still open.

B. If you are using Multiple Reporting Currencies (MRC), you can only run the Calculate Gains and Losses and depreciation programs using the standard Fixed Assets or MRC primary responsibility.

C. Once depreciation has been processed for an Asset in the current open period, you can still reverse processed transactions on those Assets unless the current period is closed.

D. Oracle Assets automatically closes the period and opens the next period for the book, whether you check or do not check the Close Period check box when you run depreciation.

Question 25 of 150

When the Initial Mass Copy program copies an Asset into a tax book, which of the following financial information comes from the corporate book?

A. Original Cost
B. Date Placed in Service
C. Capacity and unit of measure, for units of production Assets
D. All the above

All the following are not required step during
Oracle Asset setup except?

A. Leasing
B. Warranty
C. Investment Tax Credit
D. Book Control

Which of the following flex-fields allows you to
assign the same name to many Assets so you can
find similar Asset and also allow you to track your
CIP Assets?

A. Accounting Flex-field
B. Category Flex-field
C. Location Flex-field
D. Asset Key Flex-field

Which of the following programs highlights the
differences between the Asset information in
Oracle Assets and the actual Assets in physical
inventory?

A. Physical Inventory Details program.
B. Physical Inventory program.
C. Physical Inventory adjustment program.
D. Physical Inventory comparison program.

Question 29 of 150

Once the run depreciation button is checked, which of the following programs is automatically kicked off?

A. Calculated gains and losses
B. What-if-analysis
C. Asset detail report
D. Calculate tax program

Question 30 of 150

Which of the following set up step requires that you configure the workflow process?

A. System control
B. Asset Key Flex Field
C. Account Generator
D. Book Control

Oracle Assets shares organization and hierarchy information with

A. Oracle General Ledger
B. Oracle Human Resources
C. Oracle Project
D. Oracle Inventory

Question 32 of 150

You can choose to allow revaluation of accumulated depreciation in which of the following Oracle Assets form.?

A. Asset Category Form
B. System Control Form
C. Book Control Form
D. Depreciation Method Form

Question 33 of 150

If dynamic insertion is disabled which of the following windows in Oracle Asset allows you to define valid combinations?

A. Account Generator
B. System Control

C. Asset Keys
D. Asset Category

Question 34 of 150

The table name for Oracle Assets interface table is?

A. Mass_ FA_Additions
B. Mass_Additions
C. FA_Mass_Additions
D. Mass_Assets_Additions

Question 35 of 150

You can enter the default salvage value in which of the following Asset forms?

A. Asset Key
B. Book Control
C. System Control
D. Asset Category

Question 36 of 150

All the following are examples of financial adjustments you can expense or amortize except?

A. Year to Date Adjustments
B. Depreciation Method Adjustments
C. Recoverable Cost Adjustments
D. Capacity Adjustments

Question 37 of 150

You can define up to _____ segments for your Asset category flex-field.

A. 30
B. 11
C. 10
D. 7

Question 38 of 150

You can do all the following for a CIP Asset in the Source Lines window except?

A. Adjust the cost of an existing line.
B. Adjust the expense account of an existing line
C. Manually add a line
D. Delete a line for a CIP Asset

Question 39 of 150

You define automatic Asset number using which of the following Oracle Asset functionalities?

A. System Control
B. Asset Numbering Key
C. Category Flex-field
D. Asset Workbench

Question 40 of 150

Your corporate book and tax book must have the same?

A. Fiscal year
B. Asset category
C. Prorate calendar
D. Asset information

Question 41 of 150

Which of the following is true about how Oracle Asset calculates the depreciation rate of an Asset?

A. If the depreciation method uses the Asset cost, Oracle Assets calculates the fiscal year depreciation by multiplying the recoverable cost by the rate.

B. If the depreciation method uses the Asset net book value, Oracle Assets calculates the fiscal year depreciation by multiplying the recoverable net book value as of the beginning of the fiscal year, or after the latest amortized adjustment or revaluation, by the rate.
C. Oracle Assets calculates depreciation using either the recoverable cost or the recoverable net book value as a basis.
D. All the above

Question 42 of 150

Which of the following is not true if you suspend depreciation of an Asset?

A. If you suspend depreciation of an Asset when you add the Asset, Oracle Assets expenses the missed depreciation in the period you start depreciating the Asset.
B. For table and calculated methods, Oracle Assets calculates depreciation expense for the Asset based on an Asset life that includes the periods you did not depreciate it.
C. For flat-rate methods, Oracle Assets continues calculating depreciation expense for the Asset based on the flat-rate.
D. If you suspend depreciation after an Asset has started depreciating, Oracle Assets cannot catch up the missed depreciation expense in

the last period of life.

Question 43 of 150

Which of the following programs calculates depreciation expense and adjustments, and updates the accumulated depreciation and year-to-date depreciation?

A. Accumulated depreciation program
B. Calculate gain and loss program
C. Depreciation adjustment program
D. Depreciation program

Question 44 of 150

Which of the following is not true about a CIP Asset?

A. Oracle Assets automatically updates the cost to the sum of the invoice line costs after you add invoice lines to a CIP Asset using the Mass Additions process.
B. You cannot change the cost of a CIP Asset manually in the Source Lines window by entering non-invoiced items or transferring invoice lines between Assets.
C. The current cost of a CIP Asset can be positive, zero, or negative.

D. Oracle Assets defaults a cost of zero and you cannot change it.

Question 45 of 150

The process whereby Oracle Assets allows you to periodically adjust the value of your capitalized Assets due to inflation or deflation, according to rates you enter is called?

A. Reclassification
B. Revaluation
C. Translation
D. Amortization

Question 46 of 150

You can choose to copy descriptive flex-field information to the new category by checking the Copy Category Descriptive Flex-field to New Category check box on the Mass Reclassifications window.

A. True
B. False

Which of the following is not true about Depreciation book?

A. Oracle Assets defaults financial information from the depreciation book.
B. You can specify for which ledger a depreciation book creates journal entries.
C. You cannot change financial and depreciation information for an Asset in a book.
D. Each book can have independent accounts and independent depreciation rules.

Which method uses defined annual depreciation rates?

A. Calculated
B. Production
C. Flat
D. Table

Which of the following is not true about an expensed Asset?

A. Oracle Assets tracks expensed Assets.
B. The entire cost is charged in a single period to an expense account.
C. Oracle Assets depreciate expensed Assets.
D. Oracle does not create journal entries for expensed Assets.

Question 50 of 150

Which of the following conditions would keep you from performing depreciation reserve adjustments?

A. Reserve adjustments are off.
B. The fiscal year is open.
C. The depreciation book is not a tax book.
D. All the above

Question 51 of 150

A leased Asset can be capitalized if:

A. The present value of the minimum lease payment is greater than 90 percent of the initial Asset fair value.
B. No bargain purchase option
C. The lease term is shorter than 3/4 of the leased Asset's life.
D. No ownership transfer

Question 52 of 150

For each Asset and date range for which you want to enter a production amount, you must specify all the following information in the Production Interface SQL*Loader script except:

A. Production Amount
B. Asset category
C. Start date
D. Asset Number

Question 53 of 150

Which of the following uniquely identifies an Asset?

A. Asset type
B. Asset Tag Number
C. Asset Key
D. Asset category

Question 54 of 150

Oracle Assets Interface Table is called?

A. Asset Interface Table
B. Oracle Asset Interface Table
C. Mass Asset Interface Table

D. Mass Addition Interface Table

Which of the following is not a required step when preparing capital budgets?

A. Set up budget book
B. Set up corporate book
C. Set up tax book
D. Create budget Assets

During setup of the account generator in Oracle Asset, you must perform all the following steps prior to configuring your account generator except?

A. Define Unit of measure and Unit of measure classes.
B. Define Flex Field segment values and validation rules.
C. Define your Accounting Flex Field structure for each General Ledger set of books.
D. Define Category Flex Field.

You cannot use Quick Additions to add an Asset if all the following are true except?

A. Asset has sub components
B. The Asset is leased.
C. Asset life term is more than 10yrs.
D. The Asset has more than one assignment.

Question 58 of 150

Which of the following does not represent accounting entries posted from Oracle Assets to Oracle General Ledger?

A. Retirement
B. Revaluation
C. Accrual
D. Depreciation

Question 59 of 150

The client uses the flat-rate and the recoverable net book value at the beginning of each fiscal year to calculate the annual depreciation. In the second year of the Asset life (fiscal 2008), the net book value as of the beginning of the fiscal year is $12,000. Applying the 15% rate yields an annual depreciation of?

A. $3600
B. $900
C. $1000
D. $1800

Question 60 of 150

If you change the date placed in service after depreciation has been processed for an Asset, Oracle Assets treats it as a financial adjustment, and the accumulated depreciation is recalculated accordingly?

A. True
B. False

Question 61 of 150

Which of the following cannot be entered on the Depreciation Books from?

A. Asset Location
B. Depreciation method
C. Prorate convention
D. YTD depreciation

Which of the following is not true about creating your Asset fiscal year?

  A. You can set up multiple fiscal years in the fiscal year window.
  B. Fiscal year must be defined at least up to the current fiscal year.
  C. The calendar for a tax book must use the same fiscal year name as the calendar for the associated tax book.
  D. You can assign different fiscal years to your different corporate books.

All the following are optional steps in Oracle Asset setup except?

  A. Define Asset Location
  B. Define Descriptive Flex Field
  C. Define Fiscal year
  D. Define Asset Key

Question 64 of 150

You can change invoice information if the line came from another system through Mass additions.

A. True
B. False

Question 65 of 150

For which depreciation method can you use a bonus rule?

A. Table
B. Flat
C. Production
D. Calculated

Question 66 of 150

Capital asset information comes from which of the following sources?

A. Oracle Inventory
B. Oracle Receivables
C. Oracle Projects
D. Oracle Payables

Unplanned depreciation is a feature used primarily
to comply with special depreciation
accounting rules in Germany and the Netherlands.
However, you also can use this
feature to handle unusual accounting situations in
which you need to adjust which of the following
without affecting its cost?

A. Net book value and depreciation expense
B. Asset life and accumulated depreciation
C. The net book value and accumulated
   depreciation
D. Asset life and depreciation method

Question 68 of 150

Run the calculate gains and losses program to?

A. Calculate the depreciation for retired Assets.
B. Calculate gains and losses resulting from
   retirements.
C. Correct the accumulated depreciation for
   reinstated Assets.
D. Calculate Investment Tax Credit recapture for
   retired Assets in a tax book, if necessary.

Which of the following is not a Key Flex Field in Oracle Asset?

A. Accounting Key Flex Field
B. Location Key Flex Field
C. Asset Key Flex Field
D. Category Key Flex Field

Enabling the dynamic insert option in the category Key Flex Field allows a user to?

A. Create new Asset category
B. Transfer Asset from one category to another.
C. Assign accounts to the Asset categories created.
D. Disable the category Key Flex Field

Which of the following is not true?

A. You can separately track and manage detachable Asset components, while still
B. Group Asset depreciation, known as group depreciation, is computed and stored at the

individual Asset level.
C. Oracle Assets does not depreciate expensed Assets, even if the Depreciate check box in the Books and Mass Additions Prepare windows is checked for that Asset.
D. Units is used to group together identical Assets.

Question 72 of 150

Which of the following is a major limitation while implementing multiple sets of books in Oracle Assets?

A. You must retire the Asset from one depreciation book and add it to the other, if you want to transfer Assets that are in different corporate depreciation books.
B. You can run depreciation projections for several books at once if all books have same Account Flex Field structure. If they have different structures, you must project them separately.
C. Both A and B are limitations.
D. Both A and B are not limitations.

Question 73 of 150

Which of the following is not true about a warranty number?

A. Use the list of values or enter a previously defined warranty number to assign the Asset to the coinciding warranty.
B. Each warranty has a unique warranty number.
C. Setting up warranty is a required set up step in Oracle Asset.
D. You can set up and track manufacturer and supplier warranties online.

Question 74 of 150

Which of the following is true about the prorate date in Oracle Asset?

A. Oracle Assets prorates the depreciation taken for an Asset in its first fiscal year of life according to the prorate date.
B. Oracle Assets calculates the prorate date when you initially enter an Asset.
C. The prorate date is defined in the Book control window.
D. Oracle Assets determines the prorate date from the date placed in service and the prorate convention.

33

Which of the following is not correct?

A. An Asset can belong to any number of depreciation books, but must belong to only one corporate depreciation book.
B. Oracle Assets defaults financial information from the Asset category, depreciation book, and date placed in service.
C. You must assign a new Asset to a corporate depreciation book before you can assign it to any tax books.
D. You must assign Oracle Asset to a set of book before you can configure it.

Question 76 of 150

All the following will fall under major category Asset except?

A. Furniture
B. Vehicle
C. Software
D. Building

Which of the following describes an appropriate time to use Periodic Mass Copy?

A. Initializing the tax book
B. Before the corporate book accounting period closes
C. Creating budget Assets
D. After Initial Mass Copy copies Assets into the first accounting period

You can update the Oldest Date Placed in Service after assigning your fiscal calendar to the depreciation book.

A. True
B. False

Which of the following reports allows you to print Asset information, cost information, and depreciation information, as of a specified period, for a specified Asset book, balancing segment, Asset account, cost center, and Asset type?

A. Asset Inventory Report
B. Asset Maintenance Report
C. Fixed Assets Book Report
D. Capital Spending Report

Question 80 of 150

Which of the following is not true?

A. Having two-corporate book will enforce security, because each responsibility can have a different corporate book.
B. You can transfer Asset from one corporate book to another.
C. Asset transferred from one book to another will need to have a different Asset number.
D. You must use the major category Flex Field to perform capital budgeting in Oracle Assets

Question 81 of 150

Oracle Assets uses which of the following method(s) to calculate the insurance value of an Asset?

A. Market Value

B. Manual Value
C. Value as New
D. All the above

Question 82 of 150

For life-based depreciation methods, Oracle Assets uses which of the following to determine the rate table and the rate to use?

A. Depreciation method
B. Year of life
C. Prorate period
D. All the above

Question 83 of 150

Which of the following is not a Unit of Measure conversion type?

A. Inter class
B. Standard class
C. Extra Class
D. Intra class

An Asset can belong to any number of depreciation books, but must belong to only one corporate depreciation book?

A. True
B. False

Question 85 of 150

Oracle Assets uses which of the following to create journal entries?

A. Post to GL program
B. Sub ledger Accounting
C. Account generator
D. Calculate gain and loss program

Question 86 of 150

Which of the following is a Flex Field qualifier in the Asset Location Key Flex Field?

A. Country
B. State
C. County
D. City

Question 87 of 150

You can set up depreciation book using which of the following windows?

A. Book Window
B. Depreciation Window
C. Asset Category Window.
D. Asset Workbench

Question 88 of 150

Which of the following is not true about physical inventory?

A. When you check the In Physical Inventory check box, it indicates that this Asset will be included when you run the Physical Inventory comparison.
B. You cannot use the In Physical Inventory check box in the Asset Details window to override the default.
C. When you set up categories, you define whether Assets in a particular category should be included in physical inventory.
D. All the above.

All the following are Asset types except?

A. Expensed
B. Capitalized
C. Group
D. CIP

Question 90 of 150

A debit to which of the following is a subtraction from the account?

A. Depreciation expense
B. Bonus expense
C. Accumulated depreciation
D. Inter company receivables account

Question 91 of 150

This report is used to find out how much depreciation expense Oracle Assets charged to a depreciation expense account for any accounting period?

A. Reserve Adjustments Report
B. Reserve Ledger Report
C. Revaluation Reserve Balance Report

D. Fixed Asset Book Report

Question 92 of 150

All the following are depreciation ceilings type except?

    A. Expense Ceiling
    B. Investment Tax Credit
    C. Rate Ceiling
    D. Cost Ceiling

Question 93 of 150

Which of the following does not determine the depreciation rule that Oracle Asset uses?

    A. Date placed in Service
    B. Asset Category
    C. Asset Location
    D. Depreciation Book

Question 94 of 150

Which of the following is not true about a subcomponent Asset?

A. You can specify a rule in the Asset Categories window by which Oracle Assets defaults the life for a subcomponent Asset based on the category and the parent Asset life.
B. Oracle Assets automatically perform the same transaction on a subcomponent Asset when you perform it on the parent Asset.
C. You can separately track and manage detachable Asset components, while still automatically grouping them to their parent Asset.
D. The parent Asset must be in the same corporate book.

Question 95 of 150

Depreciated Asset must have a minimum value of _____ in order to continue to carry it in your book?

A. One Hundred
B. One
C. Zero
D. None of the above

Which of the following Key Flex Field in Oracle Assets carries the Asset financial information?

A. Asset Key
B. Location
C. Category
D. All the above

Question 97 of 150

Which of the following is not true about expensed items?

A. Oracle Assets does not depreciate expensed assets.
B. Oracle Asset tracks expensed items.
C. The entire cost is charged in a single period to an expense account.
D. Oracle Asset creates journal entries for them.

Question 98 of 150

When does a CIP Asset start depreciating?

A. When it is leased.
B. When it is capitalized.

C. When it is created.

D. When it is retired.

Question 99 of 150

You can do all the following in the book control screen except?

    A. Enter the fiscal year

    B. Enter Asset depreciation method

    C. Ledger Name

    D. Enter depreciation calendar

Question 100 of 150

For every Mass Addition Line, you can do all the following except?

    A. Split Mass Addition Lines

    B. Delete Mass Addition Lines

    C. Merge Mass Addition Lines

    D. Open Mass Additions Lines

Question 101 of 150

The Generate Default Account process is used to generate which of the following account(s)?

    A. Asset-level account

B. Category-level account
C. Book-level account
D. All the above

Question 102 of 150

This oracle Asset functionality allows you to copy Assets from a corporate book to a tax book?

A. Allow Mass Change
B. Allow Mass Transfer
C. Allow Mass Addition
D. Allow Mass copy

Question 103 of 150

You can open the next Asset period using which of the following functionalities?

A. Open period
B. Book Control
C. System Control
D. None of the Above

Which of the following is not true when you merge two mass additions in Oracle Asset?

A. When you merge two mass additions, Oracle Assets adds the Asset cost of the mass addition that you are merging to the Asset account of the mass addition you are merging into.
B. Oracle Assets creates journal entries for the Asset cost account for the mass addition into which the others were merged.
C. Oracle Assets records the merge when you perform the transaction.
D. When you create an asset from the merged line, the asset cost is not merged for audit purposes.

Using the Asset Workbench you can perform all the following action except?

A. Retire Asset
B. Import Asset
C. Adjust Asset
D. Transfer Asset

Question 106 of 150

_____ allows you to control access to Oracle Assets through responsibilities that you create and assign to users of the system.

    A. Security Options
    B. Profile Options
    C. User security
    D. Security Profiles

Question 107 of 150

What must you do to create capitalized Assets after the Interface Asset process?

    A. Run Mass additions post program
    B. Capitalize Asset in the Asset workbench.
    C. Post the Asset lines to General Ledger from Projects.
    D. Run the Mass additions create program.

Question 108 of 150

All the following are Asset sources except?

    A. Purchase order from Purchasing.
    B. Invoice lines from your accounts payable system.

C. Capital Assets from Oracle Projects.
D. External Asset through Mass Addition.

Question 109 of 150

Oracle Assets prorates the depreciation taken for an Asset in its first fiscal year of life according to the prorate date, the prorate date is based on which of the following?

A. The depreciation method and fiscal year.
B. The Asset prorate convention.
C. The date placed in service and the Asset prorate convention.
D. The date placed in service.

Question 110 of 150

Which of the following is not a type of depreciation method in Oracle Asset?

A. Flat
B. Prorate
C. Unit of Production
D. Table

Which of the following is used by Oracle Assets to group your Assets by non-financial information?

A. Asset Category Flex Field
B. Asset Key Flex Field
C. Book Control
D. Asset Location Flex Field

Which of the following are required segment in the Category Flex Field?

A. State Category
B. Sub- Category
C. Major Category
D. Unit Category

Which of the following is not true about Asset Key?

A. Asset Key stores some Asset financial information.
B. Asset Key can be used to group and track your CIP Assets with common Key words so

you can find them easily for inquiry or transactions.
C.   The Asset Key is a set of Key identifying information, such as project name.

Question 114 of 150

Suppose your fiscal year ends in May, you have a monthly (12 period) depreciation calendar, and you want to allocate depreciation evenly to each period in the year. You place a $10,000 Asset in service in the third period of your fiscal year (Jun-82) using a half-year prorate convention. The rate for the diminishing value (calculation basis of NBV) depreciation method is 20%. Since the Asset is using a half-year prorate convention, the prorate date is in December--the mid-point of your fiscal year. For Assets that have a prorate date at the mid-point of the fiscal year, depreciation expense for the first fiscal year of life is 50% of the amount for a full fiscal year. The depreciation for the first year (fiscal 1983) is?

A. $1000
B. $500
C. $1500
D. $2000

Question 115 of 150

Which of the following is not true about the salvage value of an Asset?

A. The percentage salvage value will be defaulted from the category default rules if the salvage value percentage is defaulted at the category level in the Asset Categories window.
B. The salvage value is calculated by multiplying the Asset cost by the default salvage value percentage.
C. You cannot enter a salvage value for credit (negative cost) Assets.
D. The salvage value cannot exceed the Asset cost.

Question 116 of 150

If you change the date placed in service after depreciation has been processed for an Asset, what step does oracle take?

A. Oracle Assets treats it as a financial adjustment.
B. You cannot change the date placed in service after depreciation has been processed for an Asset.
C. Both A and B are correct.

D. The accumulated depreciation is recalculated.

Question 117 of 150

You can carry out which of the following actions using the Tax workbench?

A. To review Asset detail, financial, and assignment information.
B. To review financial, assignment, and other asset information, perform transfers, review the purchasing or other source information, or retire the asset.
C. To assign investment tax credits and to perform reserve adjustments.
D. All the above.

Question 118 of 150

Which of the following is not true about a CIP Asset?

A. If you use Oracle Projects to track CIP Assets, you do not need to track them in Oracle Assets.
B. You can track CIP Assets in Oracle Assets, or you can track detailed information about your CIP Assets in Oracle Projects.
C. You can depreciate a CIP Asset according to

the depreciation method defined during setup of Oracle Asset.

D. Asset Key can be used to group and track your CIP Assets with common Key words so you can find them easily for inquiry or transactions.

Question 119 of 150

You can set up group asset using which of the following windows in Oracle Asset?

A. System Control
B. Asset Workbench
C. Book Control
D. Asset Category

Question 120 of 150

Which of the following is not part of the Asset close process?

A. Calculate gains and losses
B. Close current fiscal year
C. Run depreciation
D. Open new Asset period

Question 121 of 150

System Control window allows you to specify which of the following?

A. Asset numbering scheme
B. Enterprise name
C. Key Flex Field structures
D. All the above

Question 122 of 150

Employees, organizations, and other entities are partitioned by business group. If you set up more than one business group, your data will be partitioned accordingly. In addition, classifying an organization as a business group is not reversible.

A. True
B. False

Question 123 of 150

All the following are true except?

A. Oracle Assets displays the original cost of the Asset and updates it if you make a cost adjustment in the period you added the Asset.

B. The salvage value cannot exceed the Asset cost, and you cannot enter a salvage value for credit (negative cost) Assets.
C. You cannot enter zero accumulated depreciation for new capitalized Assets.
D. The recoverable cost is the portion of the current cost that can be depreciated.

Question 124 of 150

All the following are true about salvage value except?

A. The salvage value is calculated by multiplying the acquisition cost by the default salvage value percentage.
B. You can specify a salvage value as a percentage of an Asset's acquisition cost or as an amount.
C. The salvage value cannot exceed the Asset cost, and you cannot enter a salvage value for credit (negative cost) Assets.
D. You cannot perform salvage value adjustments once salvage value is calculated in Oracle Asset.

How do you determine the amount of depreciation to take in the Asset's first year of life?

A. It's dependent on the depreciation method chosen.
B. It's determined by your reporting authority's depreciation regulations.
C. Oracle calculated it based on historical data.
D. It's determined by the company senior management determines.

All of the following are true about Asset Key except?

A. Asset Key can be used to group and track your CIP Assets with common Key words so you can find them easily for inquiry or transactions.
B. Asset Key window has only one descriptive Flex Field.
C. The Asset Key is a set of Key identifying information, such as the project name and project number, that you define for each CIP Asset.
D. You must define the Asset Key Flex Field

before defining your Asset Key.

Question 127 of 150

When you run depreciation, Oracle Assets creates journal entries for which of the following?

A. Bonus depreciation accounts
B. Depreciation expense accounts
C. Accumulated depreciation accounts
D. All the above

Question 128 of 150

You can use descriptive Flex Field to capture all the following except?

A. Legacy Asset Number
B. Asset Type
C. Group Asset Number
D. Insurance company address

Question 129 of 150

You must use Detail Additions instead of Quick Additions if you need to:

A. Enter Asset category
B. Enter Asset cost

C. Enter salvage value
D. Enter the tag number

Question 130 of 150

Which step is not part of the Mass Additions process performed in Oracle Assets?

A. Mass Additions Post
B. Mass Additions Delete
C. Mass Additions Create
D. Mass Additions Prepare

Question 131 of 150

All the following are new features introduced in R12 except?

A. Sub ledger Accounting
B. Enhanced Logging for Asset Transactions and Programs.
C. Advanced Account Generator process
D. Automatic Depreciation Rollback

Which of the following is not a depreciation book type?

A. Budget
B. Accounting
C. Corporate
D. Tax

Question 133 of 150

You can enter production for a construction-in-process (CIP) Asset before you capitalize it and you can enter production for an asset before it's prorate date.

A. True
B. False

Question 134 of 150

An organization which started business in 1974 bought its first machinery equipment the 1975 and was operational within same year. It also bought an office building in 1976. The oldest Asset in its book today is the office building because the machinery equipment has been fully depreciated. In calculating the oldest date placed in service, what year should the company use?

A. 1974
B. 1975
C. 1976
D. None of the above

Question 135 of 150

To use the Physical Inventory feature in Oracle
Assets, you must load physical inventory data that
you have collected into which of the following
tables?

A. FA_ADDITION_INTERFACE TABLE
B. MASS_INV_INTERFACE TABLE
C. MASS_ADDITION_INTERFACE TABLE
D. FA_INV_INTERFACE TABLE

Question 136 of 150

_____ is the highest level of organization
and the largest grouping of employees across
which you may report?

A. Legal Entity
B. Set of Books
C. Business Unit
D. Inventory organization

Question 137 of 150

You can have maximum of _____ segment lines in the Location Key Flex Field?

A. Thirty
B. Eleven
C. Seven
D. Ten

Question 138 of 150

Which report will help you with reconciling Oracle Assets with General Ledger?

A. Budget-to-Actual
B. Reserve Summary
C. Capital Asset Detail
D. Consolidation - Unmapped Subsidiary Accounts

Question 139 of 150

Oracle Assets is fully integrated with which of the following for generating accounting entries, transaction drill down, and reporting?

A. Oracle General Ledger

B. Oracle Sub ledger Accounting
C. Account Generator
D. None of the above

Question 140 of 150

Which of the following is not part of a distribution line in Oracle Asset?

A. Location
B. Depreciation expense account
C. Supplier name
D. Employee name

Question 141 of 150

When you adjust a group or member Asset using a prior period amortization start date, Oracle Assets automatically submits which of the following programs?

A. Extended adjustment program
B. Process group adjustments program
C. Calculate gains and losses program
D. Financial adjustment program

Question 142 of 150

All the following are reasons why it is desirable to share information between applications except?

   A. Keeps users from having to enter identical data in more than one place
   B. Minimizes data synchronization problems, because each piece of data is kept in only one table.
   C. Makes information available to users in every application in the system.
   D. Minimizes time for implementation setup.

Question 143 of 150

Which of the following are Flex Field qualifiers in Oracle Asset?

   A. Minor Category and State
   B. Major category and Minor category
   C. State and Major category
   D. Minor category and Accounting

Which of the following is not true about corporate book?

A. You must assign a new Asset to a corporate depreciation book before you can assign it to any tax books.
B. Asset can have different financial information in each corporate book.
C. An Asset can belong to any number of depreciation books, but must belong to only one corporate depreciation book.
D. Each book can have independent accounts, an independent calendar, independent currency and independent depreciation rules.

Assets can be added by all the following methods except?

A. Mass Addition
B. Express Additions
C. Detailed Additions
D. Quick Additions

Question 146 of 150

Which of the following is not a type of workbench
in Oracle Asset?

A. Tax Workbench
B. Asset Workbench
C. Mass Addition Workbench
D. Invoice Workbench

Question 147 of 150

Each source line that came from another system
through Mass Additions may include
the following information except?

A. Project Number
B. Purchase Order Number
C. Account Details
D. Invoice Number

Question 148 of 150

All the following are required steps in Oracle Asset
except?

A. Define Fiscal year
B. Define Book Control

C. Define Security
D. Define System Control

Question 149 of 150

Which of the following is not true about date placed in service?

A. If you enter a date placed in service in a prior period and zero accumulated depreciation, Oracle Assets automatically calculates catch-up depreciation when you run depreciation, and expenses the catch-up depreciation in the current period.
B. You cannot change the date placed in service after depreciation has been processed for an Asset.
C. The date placed in service for CIP Assets is for your reference only. Oracle Assets automatically updates this field to the date you specify when you capitalize the Asset using the Capitalize CIP Assets window.
D. If the Asset category you entered is set up for more than one date placed in service range for this book, the date placed in service determines, which rules to use.

You cannot perform which of the following transactions on an Asset that is beyond its normal useful life?

A. Depreciation Method Change
B. Date Placed In Service Change
C. Invoice Transfers
D. All the above

Answers

1) B - By specifying a rule in the Asset Categories window by which Oracle Assets defaults the life for a subcomponent Asset based on the category and the parent Asset life.

2) B- Security Profile allows you to control access to Oracle Assets through responsibilities that you create and assign to users of the system.

3) C- You cannot revalue imported asset.

4) B- Mass Revaluation process does not use the price indexes to revalue assets.

5) D- You do not need Asset category to use the physical inventory feature; you need the location, number of units and a unique identifier.

6) B- Oracle Assets does not send journal entries

directly to the GL_JE_COLUMN table.

7) A- Cost Adjustment.

8) B- Oracle Assets defaults a cost of zero for construction-in-process (CIP) assets and you cannot change the default.

9) C- Depreciation rule is used to determine whether assets should be depreciated, the type of depreciation method to use and asset life term.

10) B- True. Oracle Assets uses the Major Category segment for capital budgeting.

11) A- False. Oracle Assets does not automatically perform the same transaction on a subcomponent asset when you perform it on the parent asset.

12) B - If the FA: Use Workflow Account Generation profile option is set to No, you must set up Sub-ledger Accounting.

13) D – You cannot transfer an asset between employees, projects, and locations. A, B, C are true.

14) A- You actually run depreciation projections for several books if all books have the same Account flex-field structure.

15) C- Price-based rate is not a depreciation method in Oracle Assets. Life-based, fixed rate and Units of Production are all depreciation methods in Oracle Assets.

16) B- State is a required segment in the Location Key Flex-field.

17) A- Units of production depreciate an asset based on quantity of that asset used during the

accounting period.

18) C- Year of life. Flat-rate depreciation methods do not determine the depreciation rate using fixed rates for year of asset life.

19) D- You can perform all the functions, add to asset, merge and split assets.

20) A- You cannot update the revaluation reserve after the period you added the asset.

21) B – You cannot load your physical inventory data into Oracle Assets using the Mass Addition interface import program.

22) D- All of them, corporate book, tax book and control tax book must be defined before you can perform mass depreciation adjustments.

23) A - MRC primary responsibility.

24) C - Account Generator requires that you configure the workflow process.

25) D- All the above.

26) D- Book control is a required step.

27) D- Asset Key Flex-field

28) D- Physical Inventory comparison program.

29) A- Calculate gains and losses program is automatically kicked off.

30) B- If you are using Multiple Reporting Currencies (MRC), you can only run the Calculate Gains and Losses and depreciation

programs using the standard Fixed Assets or
MRC primary responsibility.

31) B- Oracle Human Resources

32) C- You can choose to allow revaluation of
accumulated depreciation in the Book Control
Form.

33) C- Asset Keys

34) C- FA_Mass_Additions

35) D- Asset Category. You enter the default
salvage value in the Asset Category window.

36) A - Year to Date Adjustments

37) D- 7

38) B- Adjust the expense account of an existing line.

39) A – System Control

40) A – Fiscal Year

41) D – All the above.

42) D - If you suspend depreciation after an asset has started depreciating, Oracle Assets catches up the missed depreciation expense in the last period of life.

43) D- Depreciation program

44) B- You can change the cost of a CIP asset

manually in the Source Lines window by entering non-invoiced items or transferring invoice lines between assets.

45) B – Revaluation

46) A – True

47) C- You CAN change financial and depreciation information for an asset in a book.

48) B- Production

49) C- Oracle Assets DOES NOT depreciate expensed assets

50) D- All the above.

51) A - The present value of the minimum lease

payment is greater than 90 percent of the initial Asset fair value

52) B- Asset Category

53) B - Asset Tag Number

54) D- Mass Addition Interface Table

55) C- Set up tax book

56) D - Define Category Flex Field

57) C- You can add an asset

58) C- Accrual

59) C- $1000

60) A – True

61) A –Asset Location

62) B- Fiscal year must be defined beyond the current fiscal year

63) C- Fiscal year is a required set up step.

64) B – False. You cannot change invoice information if the line came from another system through Mass additions

65) B- Flat.

66) C- Capital Assets come from Oracle Project.

67) C- The net book value and accumulated depreciation

68) A- Calculate the depreciation for retired assets

69) A- Accounting Flex field is a Key Flex field in Oracle General Ledger.

70) A- Users can create new asset category

71) B

72) C- Both A and B limitations.

73) C- Setting up warranty is a required set up step

in Oracle Asset.

74) C- The prorate date is defined in the Book
control window. Only C is true.

75) D – Oracle Asset is one of the financial
applications that you do not need to assign it to
a set of book.

76) C- Software, it will belong to a major category
called Computer.

77) D - After Initial Mass Copy copies assets into
the first accounting period

78) B- False

79) C- Fixed Assets Book Report

80) C- Asset transferred from one book to another will need to have a different asset number

81) D- All the above

82) D- All the above

83) C- Extra class is not a unit of measure conversion type.

84) A - True.

85) B- Sub ledger Accounting creates journal entries for Oracle Assets.

86) B- State is a flex field qualifier in the Asset Location Key Flex Field.

87) A- Book Control Window.

88) B - You CAN use the In Physical Inventory check box in the Asset Details window to override the default.

89) C- Group

90) C- Accumulated depreciation. A debit to the accumulated depreciation account is a subtraction from the account.

91) B - Reserve Ledger Report.

92) C- Rate Ceiling is not a ceiling type.

93) C- Asset Location. Others play a role in the depreciation rule that Oracle Asset uses.

94) B - Oracle Assets DOES NOT automatically perform the same transaction on a subcomponent asset when you perform it on the parent asset. You have to perform those transactions independently. You can use the Parent Asset Transactions Report to review the transactions that you have performed on parent assets during a period.

95) B- One

96) C- Category

97) D- Oracle Asset DOES NOT create journal entries for them

98) B - When it is capitalized

99) B - Enter Asset depreciation method

100)   B- Delete Mass Addition Lines

101)   D- All the above.

102)   B- Allow Mass Transfer

103)   D- None of the above. When you Run the
        Depreciation program, the current period is
        close and the next period is opened.

104)   D- When you create an Asset from the
        merged line, the Asset cost is actually merged
        for audit purposes.

105)   B- Import Asset

106)   D – Security Profiles

107)   C- Post the Asset lines to General Ledger

from Projects.

108)   A- Purchase order from Purchasing.

109)   C - The date placed in service and the Asset
        prorates convention.

110)   B- Prorate

111)   B - Asset Key Flex Field

112)   C- Major Category

113)   A- Asset Key DOES NOT stores some Asset
        financial information.

114)   A- $1000

115) B - The salvage value is calculated by multiplying the acquisition cost by the default salvage value percentage.

116) C- Both A and B are correct.

117) C- To assign investment tax credits and to perform reserve adjustments.

118) C - You cannot depreciate a CIP Asset according to the depreciation method defined during setup of Oracle Asset.

119) C- Book Control

120) B- Close current fiscal year is not part of the Asset close process.

121)   D- All the above

122)   A- True

123)   C- You cannot enter zero accumulated
        depreciation for new capitalized Assets.

124)   D- You can still perform salvage value
        adjustments after salvage value is calculated in
        Oracle Asset.

125)   B- Its determined by your reporting
        authority's depreciation regulations.

126)   B- Asset Key window has more than one
        descriptive Flex Field.

127)   D- All the above.

128)   B- Asset Type

129)   C- Enter salvage value

130)   C- Mass Addition Create is a process in
        Oracle Accounts Payables (AP).

131)   C- Advanced Account Generator process.

132)   B- Accounting

133)   B- False

134)   C- 1976

135)   D- FA_INV_INTERFACE TABLE

136)   C- Business Unit

137)   B- Eleven

138)   B- Reserve Summary

139)   A- Oracle General Ledger

140)   C- Supplier name.

141)   B- Process group adjustments program.

142)   C- Makes data information available to
        users in every application in the system.

143)   C- State and Major category

144)   D- Each book cannot have independent accounts, an independent calendar, independent currency and independent depreciation rules.

145)   B – Express Additions

146)   D – Invoice Workbench

147)   C- Account Details

148)   C- Define Security

149)   B- You cannot change the date placed in service after depreciation has been processed for an Asset.

150)   D- All the above.

www.ingramcontent.com/pod-product-compliance
Lightning Source LLC
Chambersburg PA
CBHW061014050326
40689CB00012B/2640